D0193177

TO:

FROM:

KEEP IT SIMPLE

Unclutter Your Mind to Uncomplicate Your Life

JOE CALLOWAY

simple **truths**®
Small books. **BIG IMPACT.**

IGNITEREADS
spark impact in just one hour

Photo Credits
Internals: page vi, Wayne0216/Shutterstock; page viii, Nick Fewings/Unsplash; page xi, chuttersnap/Unsplash; page xii, Len Dela Cruz/Unsplash; page xiv, Warchi/iStock; page xviii, Stefan Gunnarsson/Unsplash; page xx-xxi, Billy Williams/Unsplash; page xxii, Justin Sullivan/Staff/GettyImages; page 4-5, Igor Ovsyannykov/Unsplash; page 6, Andrey_Popov/Shutterstock; page 9, Fred Pixlab/Unsplash; page 10-11, g-stockstudio/GettyImages; page 12, SNeG17/Shutterstock; page 15, Ryoji Iwatapage/Unsplash; page 16-17, Jacob Lund/Shutterstock; page 18, Cameron Spencer/Staff/GettyImages; page 21, clique images/Unsplash; page 22, Elaine Casap/Unsplash; page 24, Christian Horz/GettyImages; page 28, Casey Horner/Unsplash; page 31, patruflo/Shutterstock; page 32, phototechno/GettyImages; page 35 KieferPix/Shutterstock; page 38-39, Jeremy Lapak/Unsplash; page 40, De Visu/Shutterstock; page 43, leezsnow/iStock; page 46, T.Dallas/Shutterstock; page 64, General of the Army George Catlett Marshall, Chief of Staff. U.S. Army, 1 September 1939-18 November 1945, Image courtesy of the US Army's Center of Military History/public domain; page 67, National Archives and Records Administration/public domain; page 54, Filippo-Bacci/iStock; page 57, Bench Accounting/Unsplash; page 62, skynesher/iStock; page 64 PeopleImages/iStock; page 66, John Fitzgerald Kennedy, Aarom Shikler (1922-2015)/public domain; page 69, Great Images in NASA/public domain; page 71, Alones/Shutterstock; page 72, Nirat/GettyImages; page 76, atakan/iStock; page 80-81, Joel Peel/Unsplash; page 82, yuttana Contributor Studio/Shutterstock; page 84, Joshua Sortino/Unsplash; page 86, Jessica Ruscello/Unsplash; page 89, Steve Halama/Unsplash; page 90, Pricilla du preez/Unsplash; page 92, Raj Eiamworakul/Unsplash; page 96-97, Averie Woodard/Unsplash; page 98, lovelyday12/Shutterstock

Published by Simple Truths, an imprint of Sourcebooks, Inc.
P.O. Box 4410, Naperville, Illinois 60567-4410
(630) 961-3900
Fax: (630) 961-2168
sourcebooks.com

Printed and bound in China.
OGP 10 9 8 7 6 5 4 3 2

CONTENTS

INTRODUCTION   **V**

Simplicity and Focus   ix

Too Many Choices   xv

What Matters Most   xix

**ONCE YOU GET THERE,
YOU CAN MOVE MOUNTAINS**   **1**

What Is Most Important?   7

Begin with the Basics   13

That's What Winners Do   19

The Price We Pay   23

Blue-Tip Flame   29

THE RULES OF SIMPLICITY   **33**

Will It Make the Boat Go Faster?   41

Great Leaders Simplify   47

"This Made Him Valuable"   51

Remember Who You Are   55

Plainspoken and Clearly Defined   59

"We Help People When They're Hurt"   63

Doing the Impossible   67

Clear the Space   73

Let It Go   77

SEVEN SIMPLE TRUTHS   **83**

A FINAL THOUGHT   **99**

ABOUT THE AUTHOR   **103**

INTRODUCTION

> ## "I FEEL LIKE I AM MAKING THIS WAY MORE COMPLICATED THAN IT NEEDS TO BE."

How often do you have that thought? If you are like most people, it's probably fairly often, and the fact is that you're probably right. You are making it more complicated than it needs to be. We all are.

We live in a complicated world. How many

passwords do you have to your various accounts and devices? What does your schedule look like? Your kids' schedules? Probably pretty hectic. Are you keeping up with new technology, the daily upgrades? Too much to remember, too much to do,

too much to think about! The complications in our daily lives sometimes can seem endless.

It can all overwhelm us if we let it. But there's another way.

SIMPLICITY AND FOCUS

I've been studying and working with extraordinary organizations and top-performing individuals for over thirty years.

The most common and powerful factor in all of their successes has been the ability to simplify and focus. The two go hand in hand, because in order to get to simplicity, you have to have focus.

**FOCUS MEANS CLARITY.
CLARITY MEANS KNOWING
WHAT IS MOST IMPORTANT.**

When we are focused on what is most important, we no longer have to wade through the endless sea of choices that can stretch before us. We make better decisions. We become more effective. We experience less stress. Getting focused is the path to simplicity, and simplicity is the path to success and fulfillment.

"Simplicity is
ultimately a
matter of focus."

—Ann Voskamp

TOO MANY CHOICES

When we have unlimited choices, that's a good thing, isn't it?

Not really.

In 2000, Sheena Iyengar of Columbia University conducted a legendary marketing study on the effect of too many choices.

What she did was set up a display of jams outside a grocery store in Menlo Park, California. She rotated the display between having six flavors to choose from and twenty-four flavors to choose from.

What the study revealed was that more sales of jam were made when there were fewer choices!

Think of your own experience as a shopper. How many times have you been frozen by too many choices? Too many types of toothpaste, too many service plans with your cell provider, or too many options on that new car you're looking at—it can be overwhelming.

When we can create focus and limit our choices in life to the best ones, we make better decisions and are generally more efficient and effective.

> ## It seems the older you get, the more life comes into focus.
>
> —John C. Maxwell

WHAT MATTERS MOST

Getting to simplicity is not only more efficient and effective—it's also more fulfilling.

What if we spent most of our time, effort, and energy on those things that truly matter most?

The first step, of course, is determining what really does matter most.

With that in mind, we can simplify any problems you are facing in life.

LET'S GET STARTED.

"That's been one of my mantras—focus and simplicity. Simple can be harder than complex: you have to work hard to get your thinking clean to make it simple. But it's worth it in the end because once you get there, you can move mountains."

—Steve Jobs

Steve Jobs, September 1, 2010.

ONCE YOU GET THERE," YOU CAN MOVE MOUNTAINS

I love the words that Steve Jobs chose: *get your thinking clean to make it simple.* That's no easy task. It's much easier to have our thinking cluttered by a thousand questions and complications. It's hard work to get focused and to simplify things. But, as Jobs said, it's worth it, because when you make things simple, *you can move mountains.*

Steve Jobs is a good role model for the power of simplicity and focus.

"Any darn fool can make something complex; it takes a genius to make something simple."

—Pete Seeger

In a business that most would say is, by its very nature, incredibly complicated, Steve Jobs was able to make Apple a dominant force in the marketplace. Bill Gates once said that Jobs's ability to "focus on a few things that count" was amazing. Tim Cook, the current CEO of Apple, has said that Jobs could cut out the noise like no other. Jobs had the essential leadership skill of keeping everyone focused on what was most important.

I work with all types and sizes of businesses, and it's fascinating to see the commonalities among those that are doing well and among those that are struggling. People in a struggling business are likely to say, "You have to understand that this is a very complicated business." People in a successful business will usually say, "You know, at the end of the day, this is really a pretty simple business."

Both of them are correct because they have made it so. Successful people have the ability to make the complicated simple. That's one of the main reasons for their success.

"Simplicity is a great virtue, but it requires hard work to achieve it and education to appreciate it. And to make matters worse: complexity sells better."

—Edsger Wybe Dijkstra

WHAT IS MOST IMPORTANT?

The incredible power of simplicity begins with focus. It begins with the answer to a very simple question: What is most important?

Interestingly enough, very few people ever give careful thought to deciding what is really most important in their work or their lives. Most of us simply show up and go to work on whatever is in front of us or whatever pops up during the day. Imagine how much more effective, successful, and fulfilled we would be if we focused on doing those things that were *truly most important*, and doing them with excellence and consistency every single day?

I've had many people tell me they are frustrated because they are doing absolutely everything they can think of to succeed, but it's just not working.

Doing "everything they can think of" is most likely the root of their problem.

The winners in work, in business, and in life aren't those who do the *most* things. The winners are those people who do the *most important* things.

"You must focus on the most important, mission-critical tasks each day and night, and then share, delegate, delay, or skip the rest."

—Jessica Jackley

BEGIN WITH
THE BASICS

How do we determine what is most important?

Begin with the basics. Begin with the fundamentals. The reality is that if you succeed at the basics, you succeed in life.

Note that I'm not saying to be really good just at the basics or to be competitive on the fundamentals. I'm saying to focus and actually *win* there.

IN BUSINESS, IF YOU WIN ON THE BASICS, YOU WIN IT ALL.

There is a successful software company that has this as their mantra: "Bells and whistles wear off, but usefulness never does." This serves as a great reminder that our goal should always be to do that which creates value for our customers.

We've gotten carried away with creating "wow" factors and trying to do things that will make us different from our competition. What we forget is that the ultimate way to differentiate ourselves from the competition is by being *better* than the others!

The ultimate "wow" factor is when those you serve say, "Wow, these guys get it right every single time."

The same holds true for the rest of our lives. Get the basics right with your family, your values, your health, and your spirit, and you've created a fulfilling, happy, and successful life.

"The game has its ups and downs, but you can never lose focus of your individual goals, and you can't let yourself be beat because of lack of effort."

—Michael Jordan

Serena Williams, August 7, 2016.

THAT'S WHAT WINNERS DO

Think about the top performers in sports.

Michael Jordan is a legend in basketball because he was simply the best at the basics of basketball. His focus took "basics" to a new level.

The same has been true for Jack Nicklaus in golf, Serena Williams in tennis, Michael Phelps in swimming, and every other sports legend.

All of them were focused on being the best at what mattered most.

It wasn't easy. But they focused, excelled, and were simply better at the basics than anyone else. That's what winners do.

We win because we are focused.

We win because we do what is most important.

The rest is noise.

THE PRICE WE PAY

One of my clients, the CEO of an international agriculture business, said, "The price we pay for making things too complicated is immeasurable. It slows us down, makes for bad decisions, and scatters our efforts."

Indeed.

Think about these three parts of the price we pay for making things too complicated:

1.

Making things too complicated
slows us down.

In today's world, if we don't move quickly, opportunities disappear in the blink of an eye. The inability to focus and simplify means that we will overthink our decisions, that we will go back and forth with pros and cons and new considerations that we continue to add to the pile.

Simplicity and focus enable us to make decisions more quickly. That's a competitive advantage.

2.

Making things too complicated
makes for bad decisions.

In your experience, which solutions are the most effective? Which ideas are most likely to create success? The complicated ones? Or the simple ones?

I ask that question of my audiences, and the answer is unanimous. Everyone agrees that simple solutions and ideas are always the best. When we create complications, we increase the likelihood of failure. As we simplify, we increase the likelihood of success.

3.

Making things too complicated
scatters our efforts.

This is a very steep price that can make the most ambitious of dreams and aspirations come to absolutely nothing. When we lack focus and make it all too complicated, our efforts are watered down and weakened in their effect.

As the great inventor Alexander Graham Bell said, "Concentrate all your thoughts upon the work at hand. The sun's rays do not burn until brought to a focus."

OUR WORK IS LIKE THE SUN. IT DOESN'T BURN BRIGHT UNTIL BROUGHT TO A FOCUS.

We can always
choose to perceive
things differently.
You can focus
on what's wrong
in your life, or
you can focus on
what's right.

—Marianne Williamson

BLUE-TIP FLAME

Thinking about the power of the sun's rays when focused brings to mind another powerful metaphor about focus that has a practical application for all of us.

Imagine that you are trying to cut your way through a wall made of solid steel. The only tool you have is a flamethrower. It can project a huge flame, but when the flame hits the wall, it spreads and dissipates. You could put the flame on the wall for hours and get nowhere.

But if you trade the flamethrower for an acety-lene torch, you will achieve a more positive result. The blue-tip flame from a torch is focused and, therefore, much more powerful.

Think about your own efforts when dealing with a problem or even an opportunity. Are you scatter-ing your energy like a flamethrower, or do you have the focus and power of a torch's blue-tip flame?

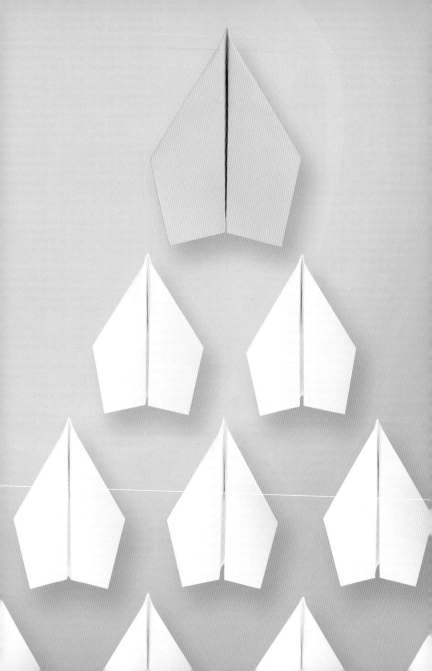

THE RULES OF SIMPLICITY

One of my clients is a national trucking company. This is a business that involves logistics, systems, schedules, and details that could easily become overwhelmingly complicated. Yet this trucking company, which is one of the largest in the country, has harnessed the power of simplicity and focus to drive consistent success for years.

They have boiled it down to three simple rules that they abide by every single day:

1. Pick it up when you said you would.

2. Deliver it when you said you would.

3. Deliver it intact and all there.

A successful drive-in restaurant chain has done much the same in getting clarity on what is most important:

1. Give customers the freshest, highest quality foods they can buy.

2. Provide meals with friendly service.

3. Serve in a comfortable, sparkling-clean environment.

These companies are great examples of the power of having a team with a shared—and simple—vision. It's actually quite easy to come up with a wordy, complicated vision, mission, or goal. It's much more challenging to create a goal that is simple and easy to understand.

Resist the temptation to overthink things. Boil it down to the essence of what matters most. We should strive to focus on the essential and minimize the rest.

"One reason so few of us achieve what we truly want is that we never direct our focus; we never concentrate our power. Most people dabble their way through life, never deciding to master anything in particular."

—Tony Robbins

So, what are the three most important things in your life, your work, or your business?

You can stop overcomplicating. Boil it down to those three most important things that you must do well every day to create success, happiness, or fulfillment. This can, and should, take some time and thought, but it's well worth the effort.

My 3 Most Important Things Are:

_____

_____

_____

"The successful warrior is the average man, with laser-like focus."

—Bruce Lee

WILL IT MAKE THE BOAT GO FASTER?

Sir Peter Blake led Team New Zealand to successive victories in the America's Cup yacht competition in 1995 and 2000. The key to this success was that Blake focused the team on one question, which they asked about everything they did: **"Will it make the boat go faster?"**

Everything they did and every decision they made had to go through the filter of "will it make the boat go faster?" This applied to the equipment they chose, their training regimen, nutrition, crew composition—everything.

The British eight-man rowing team in the 2000 Sydney Olympics adopted the same strategy of "will it make the boat go faster?" and it drove them to change everything about their strategy and daily activities. They credit winning the gold medal to this singular focus.

We can all simplify and focus using our version of that question. Look at your daily choices, activities, and decisions, and ask yourself your own version of "will this make the boat go faster?"

"Will this get me where I want to go?"

"Will this help me create positive relationships?"

"Will this assist me in reaching my sales goal?"

We all have a "boat" we want to go faster.

Be sure you are focused on doing those things that will accomplish your goals.

"

Our life is frittered away by detail... Simplify, simplify, simplify! I say, let your affairs be as two or three, and not a hundred or a thousand; instead of a million, count half a dozen, and keep your accounts on your thumbnail.

—Henry David Thoreau

"

GREAT LEADERS SIMPLIFY

Great leaders have the ability to simplify and get everyone focused on a shared goal or vision.

Years ago, I was working with a company that was struggling. The CEO called a meeting of his top leadership team to discuss how to get the company back on track. The CEO's speech was a tirade of dissatisfaction, frustration, and anger, which he ended by shouting, "Every one of you has to go back and get your people on board! That is the most important thing I expect from you, to get everyone on board!"

The CEO stormed out of the room, and everyone looked at one another in silence. You could have cut the tension with a knife. Finally, one of the senior vice presidents said what everyone was thinking: "Get on board with *what*?"

This CEO was a classic example of an ineffective leader. He had put forth so many priorities that there was no clarity. No one knew what was really important. It's so much easier to come up with twenty priorities than it is to come up with three priorities. The obvious problem with twenty priorities is that it's a faulty concept. **YOU CAN'T FOCUS ON EVERYTHING.** Having twenty priorities means having no priorities.

The more complicated you've made your business or your life, the less effective you will be. Complication freezes you into uncertainty and inaction.

Simplicity enables you to get yourself and everyone else focused on a shared vision, goal, or priority and then move forward. It's extremely hard for anyone, much less an entire organization, to focus on anything that's complicated.

George C. Marshall, circa 1945.

"THIS MADE HIM VALUABLE"

One great leader who was a master of simplicity and focus was George C. Marshall, the secretary of state for President Harry S. Truman. Almost everyone, no matter what political party they belonged to, had great respect for Marshall. It was said that he "could distinguish what was important from what was unimportant, and this made him valuable."

President Truman said that Marshall's great talent was his ability to "cut to the bone of the matter" in any situation and that he was "a tower of strength and common sense."

As the leader of the State Department, it was said that Marshall "gave a sense of purpose and direction. There was greater clarity than had ever been seen there before."

President Harry Truman shakes
hands with Secretary of State
George C. Marshall.

REMEMBER WHO YOU ARE

The value of focus and clarity is as true for a family as it is for a business.

A former business colleague once told me that his belief in the importance of clarity came from his father, who had one simple and focused message for his children, which he repeated over and over: "Remember who you are." He said his father often talked about the values that were important in their family: honesty, generosity, courage, and being ladies and gentlemen.

My colleague said that when he would go out on Saturday night with his friends when he was a teenager, his father would say to him, "Have a great time tonight, and remember who you are." That's all he had to say to remind his son to make good decisions.

What a simple, powerful lesson for all of us. When making challenging personal decisions, we can stay on course with our values if we just go by the guidance of remembering who we are.

"The ultimate in sophistication is simplicity."

—Leonard Thiessen

If you can't explain it to a six-year-old, you don't understand it yourself.

—Anonymous

PLAINSPOKEN AND CLEARLY DEFINED

Whether it's your vision, your mission, your family values, or your goals for the year, try to make it twenty words or less. Write it so that a child can understand it.

Many people have fallen into the trap of thinking that the more complicated something is, the more effective, powerful, or useful it must be. In fact, quite the opposite is true.

It's certainly true that the more plainly spoken

and clearly defined your goals are, the greater your chance of achieving them, whether they be for an individual or a team.

"WE HELP PEOPLE WHEN THEY'RE HURT"

In business, I often see mission or vision statements so wordy and full of corporate speak that they cease to have real meaning to anyone. I did consulting work with a private emergency injury facilities company. At a management meeting, the CEO had the company's three-paragraph mission statement on a screen to read aloud to the group so that everyone would be "clear on what we're all about."

When I spoke to the group later in the day, I asked if anyone could summarize their mission statement in just one sentence. No one volunteered, so I picked one woman and kept asking her to try until, with a real sense of frustration, she forcefully said, **"Look, we help people when they're hurt, okay?"**

Okay indeed. I asked the group how many of them got out of bed every morning excited and committed to achieving their three-paragraph mission statement. None of them raised their hands, including the CEO. I asked how many of them could be excited about "helping people when they're hurt." Every hand in the room went up.

There's the mission: *we help people when they're hurt.*

The power and effectiveness of such a simple statement is twofold:

- It is easy to understand.
- It motivates people on an emotional level.

Complicating our thoughts and words can take the heart out of them. We don't do great things just because we have an intellectual understanding of them; we do great things because we have an emotional commitment to them. Love, generosity, compassion, honor—these are all concepts made powerful because they don't require a great deal of thought. We simply get it. We respond emotionally to the power of simplicity.

John F. Kennedy's official portrait, painted by Aaron Shikler in 1970.

DOING THE IMPOSSIBLE

President John F. Kennedy understood the incredible power of simplicity and focus. He used it to help drive the United States to accomplish a seemingly impossible goal—putting a man on the moon.

In the early 1960s, for reasons involving the need for progress and the pressures of the Cold War with Russia, President Kennedy and his advisers determined that putting a man on the moon should become a priority for our nation.

It was much more than simply an ambitious goal: it was a goal that most people, including those in the scientific community, thought impossible.

Kennedy, in a speech on May 25, 1961, to a joint session of Congress, used the power of simplicity to rally the nation to his cause when he said:

"I believe that this nation should commit itself to achieving the goal, before this decade is out, of landing a man on the moon and returning him safely to the earth. No single space project in this period will be more impressive to mankind, or more important for the long-range exploration of space; and none will be so difficult or expensive to accomplish."

Kennedy wisely chose to simplify, rather than complicate, which enabled an entire nation to get clarity and focus on what had to be done.

John F. Kennedy, May 25, 1961.

He set a deadline: "before this decade is out."

He made the goal clear and easy to understand: "landing a man on the moon and returning him safely to the earth."

He explained why it was important: "no... project...more impressive...or more important for the long-range exploration of space."

He made clear the obstacles to overcome: "none will be so difficult or expensive to accomplish."

Kennedy could have taken hours of time and pages of words to try to convince people to join this cause. Instead, he took exactly sixty-three words not only to define the goal, but also to give the reasoning behind it and the challenges it imposed.

On July 20, 1969, Neil Armstrong became the first man to set foot on the moon. His statement to the world as he stood on the moon's surface was elegant and inspiring in its simplicity: "One small step for man, one giant leap for mankind."

Ten words that went down in history.

Ten words that expressed more than one hundred books could have.

The old saying "less is more" became an old saying because it is so undeniably true.

CLEAR THE SPACE

Have you ever looked in your refrigerator for something that you know is there, but you just can't find it? You move the pickles, you take out the mayonnaise, you look behind the leftover meat loaf, but you still can't see what you're looking for. Finally, you are hit with a blinding flash of the obvious: you need to clean out the refrigerator!

In life, we periodically need to simplify and get focused by doing a version of cleaning out the refrigerator. One of the most powerful things we can do is let go of those things that are complicating our lives and getting in the way of what we really want.

My friend, the great business thinker and educator Nido Qubein, once said that in addition to having a to-do list, he also had a "to let go of" list. There is great wisdom and power in this idea, as you can't accomplish the things you aspire to until you clear the space for them to happen.

For years, I have worked with groups and individuals on the concept of "let it go" and the impact it can have on efficiency, effectiveness, and quality of life.

What's interesting is that most of us intuitively already know what we should let go of. The challenge is to take action to end negative patterns, habits, or relationships that are getting in our way.

"

The greatest step
toward a life of
simplicity is to
learn to let go.

—Steve Maraboli

LET IT GO

A first step toward simplifying and getting focus in our lives is to make a "let it go" list and take action on it. In working with thousands of people on these lists, I have found these items to be the top ten things people have identified that they need to let go:

I NEED TO LET GO OF:

- Waiting for someone else to fix it.
- Worrying about things over which I have no control.
- Trying to make something work that's never going to.
- Avoiding that person who I know I need to have a conversation with.
- Trying to do everything perfectly.
- Wasting time with negative people.
- Hoping that the person causing the problem will somehow miraculously change.
- Putting off the decision I know I should make right now.
- Procrastinating.
- Dwelling on what's wrong rather than making it right.

Some of the things on this list may apply to you. Whether they do or not, now is the time for you to make your own "let it go" list and clear the space for you to get focused on what's truly important and productive in your life.

Many of the "let it go" items have to do with hesitating or simply not moving ahead with what we know we should do. We must let go of that hesitation. My dear friend, successful advertising agency CEO Arnie Malham, says, "If it's worth doing, it's worth doing wrong." What he means is that if we wait until we feel that we'll do it perfectly, we'll never do it, and if we never do it, then it's an opportunity lost. Arnie says, "Do it. Do it wrong. Then do it better."

"Until one is committed, there is hesitancy, the chance to draw back, always ineffectiveness. Concerning all acts of initiative (and creation), there is one elementary truth the ignorance of which kills countless ideas and splendid plans: that the moment one definitely commits oneself, then Providence moves too. A whole stream of events issues from the decision, raising in one's favor all manner of unforeseen incidents, meetings, and material assistance, which no man could have dreamt would have come his way. I have learned a deep respect for one of Goethe's couplets: 'Whatever you can do or dream you can, begin it. Boldness has genius, power, and magic in it.' Begin it now."

—William H. Murray

SEVEN SIMPLE TRUTHS

I have spent more than thirty years working with successful leaders and top performers in all walks of life and in all kinds of businesses. Perhaps the greatest lesson I've learned from this experience is this: there are no *secrets of success*. What it takes to succeed is known by virtually everyone, and it rarely involves anything particularly complicated. Success is simple. That does not mean, however, that it is easy.

Here are seven simple truths that will help you create success in your own life and work:

1. THE GOLD STANDARD

I will do what I promised. It doesn't matter what else is going on. It makes no difference whether I'm in a bad mood, having a lousy day, or dealing with ten problems at once.

I will do what I promised. What's more, I will do it every single time.

This is the Gold Standard. To be able to say "you can count on me" and back it up. There is no value simpler, or more powerful, than keeping your promises.

2. DON'T GET STUCK IN WHAT USED TO WORK

We all recognize the value of experience. It's useful to know what has worked in the past. But I

believe that one of the greatest enemies of future success is past success.

If I am successful, that means I know what used to work. I can tell you how to succeed up until today. In business, current success means you can compete and win in markets that no longer exist—because the marketplace changes every day.

What got you to your current level of success

just may be what's keeping you from getting to the next level. Be willing to let go of what used to work.

Be open to what will work next.

3. BE BETTER TOMORROW THAN YOU WERE TODAY

I'll often ask an audience, "How many of you believe that in order to stay competitive, you have to be better tomorrow than you were today?" Every hand in the room goes up. Everyone says that they absolutely believe in the idea of constant improvement. There's no debate about it. Constant improvement is a requirement.

And yet when I ask the question, "So what did you do last Thursday that made you better than you were on Wednesday?" no one has an answer.

The simple concept of continuous improvement gets more lip service than just about any idea around. It's very easy to talk about, but not so easy to do.

The key is to build a focus on improvement into everything you do, not as a project, but as a daily process. How can I make the next meeting more efficient and effective? What will I do in my next sales call to make it more likely to result in a sale?

Continuous improvement isn't an option anymore. It's a requirement.

4. WIN INSIDE THE BOX

To be innovative and creative, we need to think outside the box. But we can get so carried away with new ideas and thinking outside the box that we often miss the greatest opportunity for improvement. Top performers know that true innovation creates value and that improving on the basics can create the greatest value of all.

Sometimes you need to get back inside the box.

Set the goal of being so good at the basics that you are cutting edge.

Certainly, we should be creative. Of course we

want to think outside the box. Just be sure that you're winning inside the box.

5. EXPECT TO CONNECT

Your willingness to connect with people is one of the simplest and most important success factors in your life. It comes down to focus and intention. If you want to connect, you will.

Think about every person in the past three days that has made a favorable impression on you. It may have been the checkout clerk at the grocery store, one of your customers, an acquaintance you spoke with on the telephone, or a stranger you simply passed on the street. What was the common factor in every one of those interactions? A connection was made. It may have lasted no more than a few seconds, but a real connection was made.

The older I get, the more I realize the absolute truth that the quality of my life is largely determined by the quality of my relationships. I expect not only to connect, but also to make positive, productive connections. I have learned the value of a smile to a stranger and the wisdom in truly listening to someone's problem.

It's about as simple as any idea could be, but if you go into each day with the intention that you expect to connect, your likelihood of success, happiness, and fulfillment are sure.

6. BE YOU—WE HAVEN'T SEEN THAT

If you've ever felt that you should know more than you do, be smarter or more talented, or be more than you really are in any way whatsoever, you're not alone. To one degree or another, we're all making it up as we go along. Don't let that slow you down one bit. You're in good company.

The late, great poet Maya Angelou once said, "Each time I write a book, every time I face that yellow pad, the challenge is so great. I have written eleven books, but each time I think, 'Uh-oh, they're going to find me out. I've run a game on everybody, and they're going to find me out.'"

Here's a woman who was absolutely brilliant, successful, and universally respected, and she had the same insecurities as you and me.

The trick is to figure out what you're all about and run with it. Forget about who you think you're *supposed* to be.

Who *are* you? Stop trying to be some idealized version of somebody else. If you're trying to be Bill Gates, Lady Gaga, Oprah Winfrey, or Warren Buffett, give it up. It's already been done by the originals; we have already seen what they can do.

Be you. We haven't seen that.

7. WHATEVER HAPPENS IS NORMAL

Many years ago, I worked with a man who gave me some of the most valuable advice I've ever heard. We were working together in a business that was full of ups and downs and having to deal with the unexpected.

The advice he gave was wonderfully simple: "Whatever happens is normal."

What he meant was that in business, just as in life, we are going to have to deal with the unexpected, the unanticipated, and the unfair. Those who deal most successfully with all of it are the ones who have the attitude that indeed **whatever happens is normal.**

That doesn't mean that whatever happens is acceptable or pleasant. But it does mean that changes and surprises are a part of life, and we can choose to either roll with the changes or have the changes roll over us.

I would tell
the seventeen-
year-olds to be
proud of who you
are. Don't try to
change yourself
for others.

—Lea Michele

"The more simple we are, the more complete we become."

—Auguste Rodin

A FINAL THOUGHT

Getting focused and making things simple can look like an unattainable goal. But you can do it. Any of us can.

The key is to know that progress happens one small step at a time. It begins with knowing that we may not always control the circumstances around us, but we always have total control over our perception of those circumstances.

A colleague of mine had a simple and brilliant

philosophy about dealing with problems and challenges: "There is another way of looking at this."

Although I teach the principles of focus and simplicity to people and businesses around the world, I still sometimes find myself feeling stuck and frustrated with my own inability to deal with changes, complications, and challenges.

Then I remember: **"There is another way of looking at this."** I take a deep breath, take a mental step back, and look at my challenge with new eyes.

Once I let go of old habits and patterns, which usually involve making things way too complicated, I can begin to focus and see simple solutions that create great opportunities.

> **HERE'S TO YOUR FINDING THE SIMPLE THINGS IN LIFE THAT MAKE IT ALL WORTHWHILE.**

"

When you have
exhausted all
possibilities,
remember this:
you haven't.

—Thomas Edison

ABOUT THE
AUTHOR

Joe Calloway is a leading performance expert who helps great companies get even better. He helps individuals and organizations focus on what is truly important, inspires constant improvement, and motivates people to immediate action.

Joe has been a business author, coach, and speaker for thirty years, and his client list reads like an international Who's Who in business, ranging from companies like Coca-Cola and IBM to Cadillac and American Express.

Joe is the author of six groundbreaking business books: *Be the Best at What Matters Most: The Only Strategy You'll Ever Need*; *Becoming a Category of One: How Extraordinary Companies Transcend Commodity and Defy Comparison*; *Indispensable: How to Become the Company That Your Customers Can't Live Without*; *Work Like You're Showing Off: The Joy, Jazz, and Kick of Being Better Tomorrow than You Were Today*; *Never by Chance: Aligning People and Strategy through Intentional Leadership*; and *Magnetic: The Art of Attracting Business*.

Joe is a popular speaker for business meetings and events and has been inducted into the Speaker Hall of Fame.

Joe has had articles published in more than one hundred magazines, including *Entrepreneur Magazine*, *SUCCESS*, *CIO*, *American Way*, *Industrial Supply*, *American Bar Association—The Young Lawyer*, and *Speaking—The Magazine of*

Professional Speaking.

Joe has been interviewed on dozens of media and Internet outlets, including Bloomberg Business Television, BlogTalk Radio, *The Tennessean*, Knowledge Center, *Human Business Way*, *The Rory Vaden Show*, *Blubrry*, *Podbay*, *PMA Newsline*, *American Perspective*, *The Business Builders Show*, TalkZone, Personal Life Media, *The Bob Burg Show*, *RainToday*, *The Jeff Korhan Show*, Networking Insight, WiseBread.com, and many more.

Joe lives in Nashville, Tennessee, with his wife, Annette, and his daughters, Jessica and Cate.